Finding Happy

A Motivational Journey

Motivation from the Mancave

Andre Bobo

Copyright © 2024

All rights reserved. No part of this book may be used or reproduced by any means, graphic, electronic, or mechanical, including photocopying, recording, taping, or by any information storage retrieval system, without the written permission of the publisher except in the case of brief quotations embodied in critical articles and reviews.

FINDING HAPPY

A Motivational Journey

Introduction

In the mind is where our physical reality begins to form. We have countless thoughts daily that play just as important roles as diet and exercise. The way we think has a direct impact on the life we choose to create. Whatever we continue to manifest is a direct reflection of what we believe. A centered approach aimed at taking control over your thoughts is perhaps one of the most important things we can do for a healthy and happy life. If we can first imagine the dream, then we have seen a glimpse of what is possible. If we focus on executing this dream, it shall be done.

While mental imagery can be a highly effective tool in manifesting our goals, writing down our thoughts can be therapeutic, and it offers an extra level of accountability. Doing so makes it possible to increase clarity and monitor our progress as we pursue these outcomes. When we combine this with positive affirmations, it triggers the proper response to jumpstart our day and refocus our actions. Therefore, we put ourselves in a great position to have productive and successful outputs that all began with internal thought.

This devotional has been designed to serve as a building block for tranquil ideas and ease of unnecessary burdens. It consists of both conventional and unconventional motivational quotes that will inspire you to boldly press forward. The words written inside this journal are meant to lessen your worries with practical ideas that will simply resonate. Once these ideas are consumed, jot down how you wish to use them to manifest a healthier, happier you.

I hope that you enjoy this journey as much as I enjoyed creating the conduit in which you may set sail. I am elated at your decision to pursue an opportunity to be the happiest version of yourself. You have taken a very important step to change your reality by modifying how you think. This is only the beginning, and I hope it is as helpful for you as it has been for me. I sincerely hope that with the help of this devotional; you all FIND HAPPY. Thank you!

-Andre

Date_____

"There is no need to worry about TOMORROW or stress about YESTERDAY. Do your best with TODAY for today is all we have."

Date_____

"Stop trying to change people. Instead, try to understand them better or leave it alone altogether. You're not going to change a person; only they can do that."

Date_____

"Most people only love the truth that supports a narrative that makes them comfortable. If the truth creates discomfort, a person will likely fight it or ignore it."

Date_____

"In this grand scheme of life, truth is not as important as belief. What someone believes will lead to action whether that belief is true or false."

Date_____

"A happy life looks different for everyone. Projecting our specific ideas of happiness on one another becomes confusing. Make the best of YOUR life!"

Date_____

"Your most valuable asset is time. Use it wisely."

Date_____

"Accountability is a superpower."

Date_____

"Make it a habit to practice things that produce confidence. If it makes you feel strong or capable, do it more."

Date_____

"As long as you have a little more time; you have all the time you need."

Date_____

"It is NOT a requirement to allow someone to mistreat you; so DON'T."

Date_____

"Just SAYING you are ok is not a substitute for BEING ok; but it can be a good start."

Date_____

"Patience will always reveal what hurry does not."

Date_____

"The one ingredient you will always need is BELIEF."

Date_____

"Stay out of the past, you can't change anything there. Try not to dwell too much in the future, you will miss your moment."

Date_____

"Experiences are what shape people. Extend grace because we do not know
what someone else has been through."

Date_____

"Some days you will catch the red lights and some days the green ones.
That's just life. Either way, you're doing great, keep going."

Date_____

"Do something kind for someone today; it will change your mood."

Date_____

"Never allow another's bad habits to rub off on you. Continue to be great even when they are not."

Date_____

"Take some time to identify what happiness means to you and then pursue THAT every day."

Date_____

"Most people would not have much to talk about without complaints; do not be like most people."

Date_____

"Be excited about life so you can be a witness to how exciting life can be."

Date_____

"The most comfortable place for pity is inside the mind of someone not willing to grow."

Date_____

"Take nothing for granted; each experience is at least one small part of the journey."

Date_____

"Feeling sorry for yourself changes absolutely nothing for the better."

Date_____

"You cannot control the opinions of others. However, you can control your response."

Date_____

"Life is one thing, but quality of life is EVERYTHING."

Date_____

"The only other person you should ever imagine being is a better version of yourself."

Date_____

"Worry cannot exist in the presence of faith. Worry is the failure of faith."

Date_____

"Everyone has the potential to accomplish great things. The problem is, not everyone is aware of that."

Date_____

"Your past ceases to imprison you after you've dealt with it properly. Process it and move on."

Date_____

"Try to see yourself the way someone who adores you sees you."

Date_____

"Today is your audition for tomorrow. How are you doing so far?"

Date_____

"The mind is where your reality is conceived. Focused thoughts become physical things."

Date_____

"Many times, people are not truly excited about your accomplishments, they are intimidated by them. No worries, that is not your issue. Keep going!"

Date_____

"Feelings are real, but they are not always right. Take a deep breath, acknowledge them and move on."

Date_____

"It is hard to improve yourself if you are dishonest about who you are. Take an honest assessment and get to work."

Date_____

"Complaining is another form of awareness; the only thing it does is identify that a problem exists. However, change eagerly responds to your action."

Date_____

"Many people may not like to see you without stress, disappointment, anger, concern, worry, or unease. Give them a show they didn't think they wanted to see!"

Date_____

"Begin every day in gratitude. Being grateful is a gift of life."

Date_____

"Your peace should always be a priority."

Date_____

"See people for who they are, not who you would like them to be."

Date_____

"Tomorrow owes you nothing if you do nothing today."

Date_____

"Never WORRY about the outcome; ENVISION it."

Date_____

"The opinions of others may often be unfavorable; luckily for us, people are not the source of our favor."

Date_____

"Today, go easy on you. Do not overthink it. Take the time to be grateful for the experience of existence. You are a success. Humanity is not easy. Be proud of you"

Date_____

"Go ahead and start that thing you have been putting off; it's going to work."

Date_____

"Never allow anyone to make you feel guilty about being the best version of yourself."

Date_____

"Remember, without you in that dark place, some people would get lonely. Misery does indeed love company."

Date_____

"Keep telling yourself all the great things you desire to hear from others.
YOUR belief in you is so much greater than anyone else's belief in you"

Date_____

"Today could be the day that everything changes for the better; BE PRESENT"

Date_____

"Surround yourself with people who want more for you than they want from you."

Date_____

"You will never make them all happy, but never forget to make yourself happy."

Date_____

"Push through; there is so much power in not giving up."

Date_____

"Losing someone special feels like the time was not enough; it wasn't. But do not be too tough on yourself with guilt of what could have been; it will not change anything. You are human and you are doing the best you can."

Date_____

"Once you truly understand the value of peace, you will indeed choose it."

Date_____

"Being in love is amazing; but being OF love is unbreakable."

Date_____

"What is SHOWN over time is more important than words SPOKEN in a moment."

Date_____

"If you don't change anything, don't expect anything to change."

Date_____

"Showing someone how much they mean to you does wonders for your spirit. Try it!"

Date_____

"If you can imagine it, then you have seen a glimpse of what could be."

Meet the Author

Andre "Southside Dre" Bobo, hails from Greenville, South Carolina, but currently calls Atlanta, Georgia, home. He is a father, son, brother and friend to an amazing community who supports him in all his endeavors. As an Analyst by trade, his true passion lies in writing, creating and curating content that connects people. He is the host of the podcast "ManCave with Southside Dre," where he facilitates thought-provoking conversations with community leaders, fathers, businessmen, and businesswomen. The show serves as a safe space for unfiltered and untapped dialogue, delving into edgy topics that spark meaningful discussions. Dre brings a unique blend of analytical insight and professional creative flair to his podcast endeavors. He challenges the norm while offering ideas to offset herd mentality. Currently working on several books, Andre has also begun producing short films and other television shows to be released soon. His inspiration has always been to "be the change he would like to see." As you continue to explore this journal, please be on the lookout for all things ManCave and pertaining to the Southside Dre brand. We appreciate you all and thank you very kindly!

www.ingramcontent.com/pod-product-compliance
Lightning Source LLC
Chambersburg PA
CBHW052111080125
20078CB00042B/699